the later years of **METROPOLITAN STEAM**

the later years of
METROPOLITAN STEAM

H. C. CASSERLEY

D. BRADFORD BARTON LTD

Frontispiece: One of the very fine 4-4-4T express engines, No.108, built in 1920, with a down train to Aylesbury, near Chorley Wood on 2 June 1934.

© copyright D. Bradford Barton ☐ 779/2 DB ☐ IRRC ☐ ISBN 0 85153 3272 ☐ Photoset in Bembo and printed offset litho by Mackays of Chatham Plc for the publishers D. Bradford Barton Ltd, of Trethellan House, Truro, Cornwall

The north end of Aylesbury station, in May 1936, with 4-4-4T No.107, about to depart for Verney Junction.

introduction

For a brief treatise on and pictorial record of 'the later years of Metropolitan Steam' a convenient and rather obvious commencing date is the year 1925, when on 5 January electric working over the 'main line' into rural Buckinghamshire, with its already established outer 'commuter' service, much publicised under the pseudonym 'Metroland', was extended from Harrow northwards to Rickmansworth. It was at this latter place that the change-over from steam to electric traction was to remain for the next 36 years, until 9 September 1961. At the latter date locomotive-hauled trains, which had by this time come within the ramifications of the London Transport Board, were replaced by multiple units as far as Amersham, the final limit of electrification; and beyond this the Metropolitan & Great Central Joint Line then became part of the nationalised British Railways system.

The Metropolitan Railway, together with the associated Metropolitan District, which also receives brief mention in these pages, had of course started life in the 1860s as an underground railway serving the area of Central London and which had been electrified as long ago as 1905. Briefly to recapitulate the history of the country extensions, it may be recalled that Rickmansworth had been reached in 1887, Chesham (which was a branch) in 1889, and Aylesbury in 1892, where the line joined up with the Aylesbury & Buckingham Railway. The latter had been opened in 1868 and taken over by the Metropolitan in 1891. There were also branches to Uxbridge (1904), Watford (1925) and Stanmore (1932), but the last two were electrified from the start and Uxbridge almost entirely so. The terminus of the Aylesbury & Buckingham was at Verney Junction on the LNWR Bletchley to Oxford line, a small rural outpost in the midst of a sparsely populated area, hardly even boasting a village, as it remains to this day. Small wonder that the station was entirely closed in 1968, and the Metropolitan line is now completely abandoned. It is difficult to imagine that it once enjoyed a service of through trains (one even conveying a Pullman Car) to Baker Street in the heart of London. In 1898 the Aylesbury & Buckingham was joined at Quainton Road by the Manchester, Sheffield & Lincolnshire extension to London, when this became the Great Central. The whole line beyond this point and Harrow was run on a joint basis by the Metropolitan & Great Central Joint Committee, each railway operating its own trains from Baker Street and Marylebone. Maintenance of permanent way, stations, buildings and signalling were carried out by the two railways — extending through into LNER days, for alternate five yearly periods. South of Harrow both companies had their own individual tracks.

No account of the Metropolitan would be complete without a mention of the Brill branch, that completely rural oddity of a busy city railway system, and which survived until 1935. Originally a private venture on the part of Duke of Buckingham, this was opened in 1871, known as the Wotton Tramway (later the Oxford & Aylesbury Tramroad) although it never came within a dozen miles of the former city, and was acquired by the Metropolitan in 1899. It left the main line at the aforementioned Quainton Road, now well-known as an active steam centre with a large collection of engines.

In 1925 the Metropolitan maintained a stock of about 35 steam locomotives necessary for its service over the main line, both passenger and freight, plus the Chesham and Brill branches and various departmental duties centred on its main headquarters at Neasden. The last new engines to be built were six 2-6-4Ts, from Armstrong Whitworth in 1924, incorporating parts of Maunsell's 'Woolwich' 2-6-0s of SE&CR design. These had been built by the Government for war purposes and had now become redundant. Their arrival enabled an equivalent number of the remaining old Beyer Peacock 4-4-0Ts, originally 66 of them in all, to be disposed of. Several of these had been retained after the Inner Circle electrification of 1905, and a small number were still left for the Brill branch and other lighter miscellaneous duties until 1936.

In 1933 the Metropolitan Railway was incorporated into the London Passenger Transport Board, which included the District Railway, the London Underground network, plus the various bus and tramway systems. From 1 November 1937 the LNER assumed entire control of steam working north of Rickmansworth, and the 'main line' engines, the 0-6-4Ts, 4-4-4Ts and 2-6-4Ts, became part of the LNER stock and were transferred to that company's running shed at Neasden on the opposite side of the line to the former Metropolitan premises and power station. A few departmental engines were retained by London Transport and were given new numbers.

The following table gives a brief history of Metropolitan locomotives in existence from 1920 onwards:

The illustrations are all from the author's own camera,
except where otherwise credited.

Class	Type	Built	Met. Nos.	LT. Nos.		Disposal
A and B (survivors of the original engines Nos. 1-66)	4-4-0T	1864-85	7, 18, 22, 23, 24, 26, 27 41, 42, 44, 46, 48, 49 (See Note A)	L45 (23)		Some sold, others scrapped. (No.23 retained for preservation)
C	0-4-4T South Eastern Railway Stirling design	1891	67-70			No.69 sold about 1920, others scrapped
D	2-4-0T	1894-5	71-76			Some sold, 1920 onwards, others scrapped
E	0-4-4T	1896-1901	1 77-82 (see Note B)	L44 (1) L46-L48 (77, 80, 81)		Scrapped 1935-1962 (L44 preserved at Quainton Road)
Unclassified	0-6-0ST	1897-9	101, 102	L53, L54		Scrapped 1961
F	0-6-2T	1901	90-93	L49-L52		Scrapped 1957-1962
				LNER No. (1937)	LNER No. (1946)	
G	0-6-4T	1915	94-97 (see Note C)	6154-6157	9076 (6155) 9077 (6156)	Scrapped 1943-1948
H	4-4-4T	1920	103-110	6415-6422	7511 (6416) 7512 (6417)	Scrapped 1942-1947
K	2-6-4T	1924	111-116	6158-6163	9070 (6158) 9071 (6160)	Scrapped 1943-1948

Note A   Survivors of the original series of 66 engines, Nos.1-18 (Class A) and 19-66 (Class B).

Note B   One of these engines received the number 1 as the original Beyer Peacock 4-4-0T had been scrapped after being involved in an accident.

Note C   *Lord Aberconway, Robert H. Selbie, Charles Jones* and *Brill;* the only Met engines to bear names since the earliest days (the original eighteen of the Beyer Peacock 4-4-0Ts being named when first built).

Almost all of the remaining Beyer Peacock 4-4-0Ts were taken out of service in 1936 following the closure of the Brill branch, the working of which had become the principal duty of the few survivors. No.23 was alone in lasting long enough to acquire the new identification of 'London Transport' consequent on the incorporation of the Metropolitan Railway into the London Passenger Transport Board in 1933. It is seen here at Wood Siding on 22 June 1935. Other views in this picturesque setting appear on pages 72-74. No.23 was fortunately retained by the LPTB and was eventually set aside for preservation. Restored to original condition, it was at first housed in Clapham Museum (see page 96) but may now be seen in the London Transport Museum at Syon Park, Brentford.

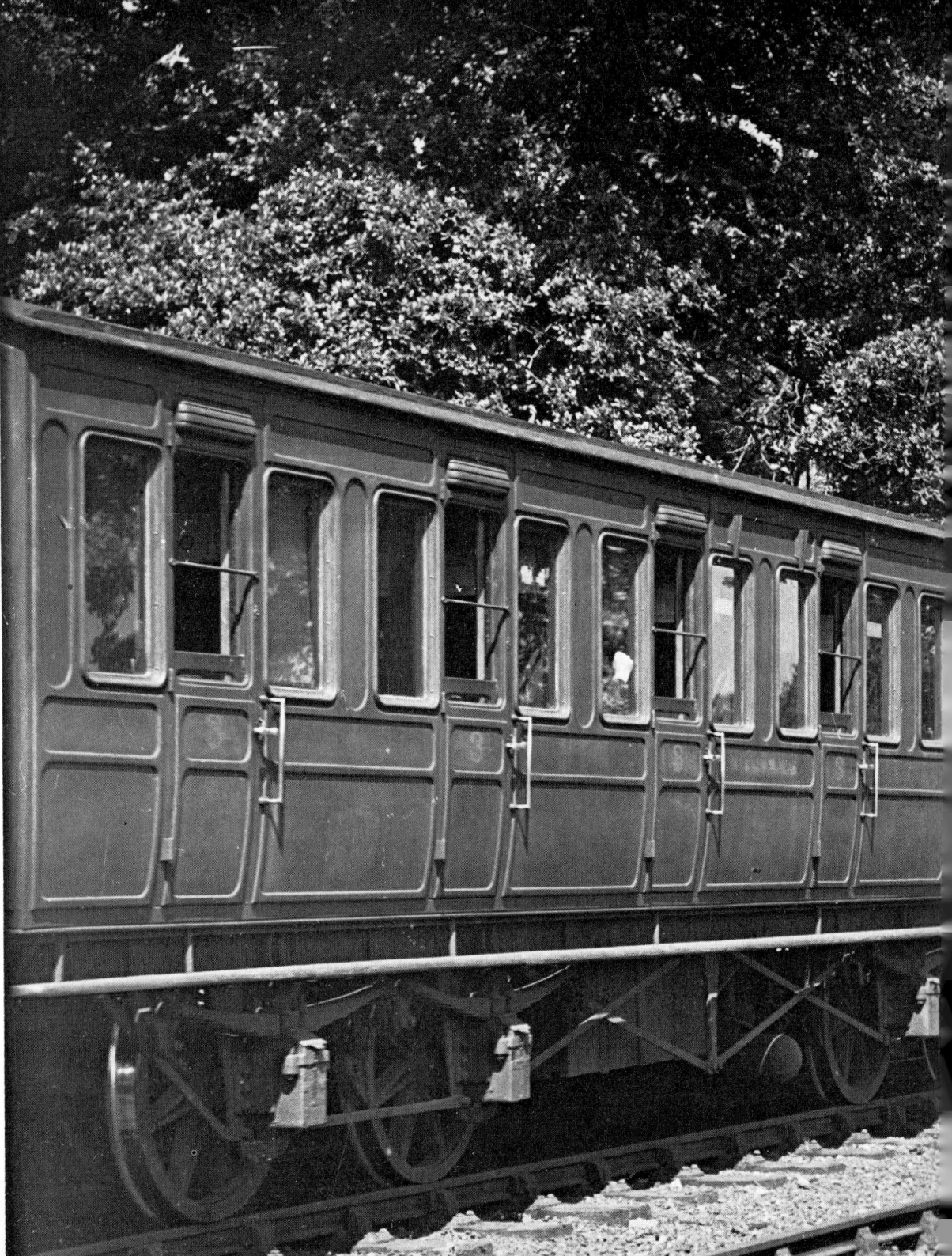

Several of the 4-4-0Ts latterly in service, indirectly displaced by the arrival of new 2-6-4Ts in 1924, were to be found at Neasden Yard in June 1925 awaiting disposal. These included No.7, which was sold to the Mersey Railway in Liverpool for departmental duties where, as Mersey No.2, it was to last until 1939. No.7 was one of the original batch of eighteen engines, which at first were given names, this one being *Orion*.

Another one, No.44, was sold to the Pelaw Main Colliery, in Durham, together with Nos.24 and 26. It passed into the hands of the National Coal Board in 1947 and survived until December 1948. Also present on the occasion of this photograph was No.22, which was disposed of in 1926 to the then associated but still independent Metropolitan District Railway, where it became No.35 (see page 52).

Another later survivor was No.27, photographed at Neasden on 11 March 1933, before being scrapped in the same year. In the background is part of the power station, from which the railway provided its own supply of current for its extensive electrification.

No.L45 (late No.23) at the Lillie Bridge depot of the former District Railway on 14 July 1939.

Class E 0-4-4T No.1, built at Neasden in 1898, was so numbered to replace the original 4-4-0T which had been broken up after being involved in an accident; photographed at Chalfont, April 1933.

No.1 again, after passing into the hands of the newly-created London Passenger Transport Board in 1933, at Neasden on 11 July 1936. This engine was later renumbered L44 in a new series created by the LPTB (see page 19).

Another E class 0-4-4T, carrying the Metropolitan coat of arms on the bunker, at Neasden in April 1927. It is resplendent in the livery of Metropolitan engines — a fine rich red, somewhat similar to, but of a darker shade than the well-known crimson lake of the Midland. Lining-out was in black edged with yellow. Metropolitan engines were maintained in superb spick and span condition at this period.

No.81 having its smoke box cleaned out at Neasden on 11 March 1933, exhibits a slightly different style of painting with the number on the bunker in lieu of on the tank side. This view shows the old corrugated iron shed later replaced by the more modern structure illustrated on page 58.

No.81 was one of the four Class E 0-4-4Ts which survived to become Nos.L44, L46, L47 and L48 in the London Transport list; L48 was photographed at Neasden on 4 October 1958.

No.1 again, which became LT No.L44, on a steam rail tour at New Cross Gate on 1 October 1961. It was by this date the only surviving Metropolitan engine in working order and was later acquired by the Quainton Road Society. It is now at the premises at Quainton Road awaiting restoration and is one of only two former Metropolitan locomotives still in existence, the other being 4-4-0T No.23 (see page 96).

The four 0-6-2Ts were later renumbered L49-L52 by the LPTB. No.L49 was photographed at Neasden on 22 June 1947. These engines were scrapped between 1957 and 1962.

Class F consisted of four 0-6-2Ts, Nos.90-93, built by the Yorkshire Engine Co in 1901 for general freight duties over the main line. No.93 is seen on an up train near Chorley Wood on 2 June 1934.

Shortly before being taken over by the Transport Board in 1933, an abbreviated designation M E T replaced the full wording on the tank sides, but so far as is known, only two engines received this treatment before the words 'London Transport' began to appear. One of them was 0-6-2T No.91, seen here at Neasden on 11 July 1936. The other was 4-4-4T No.105, illustrated on pages 24/25.

Eight very fine 4-4-4Ts were built by Kerr Stuart & Co in 1920 for express work between Harrow (later from Rickmansworth) and Aylesbury or Verney Junction, on which duties they performed very satisfactorily. Later they were gradually replaced by GCR A5 4-6-2Ts and other types when these workings were taken over by the LNER. No.104 is seen at Aylesbury on 2 May 1936.

No.109 with an up train to Baker Street near Chorley Wood on 2 June 1934.

As already mentioned, one of the two engines to receive the abbreviated MET on the tank sides was No.105, seen here with a down train near Chorley Wood, 2 June 1934.

After being taken over by the LNER in 1937, Metropolitan engines went to Stratford for major overhaul. The 4-4-4Ts became Nos.6415-6422 in the LNER list, and No.6415 (late No.103) was in Stratford works on 12 March 1938 having just been repainted in LNER livery.

No.6415 at work near Wendover, on 8 July 1939.

During the early 1940s, the 4-4-4Ts were drafted away to the Nottingham area. No.6416 is seen here at Edwinstowe on 8 May 1946, on the former Lancashire, Derbyshire & East Coast Railway — a line which never reached either Lancashire or the East Coast, its limits being Chesterfield in the west and Lincoln in the east. It was absorbed by the Great Central, this becoming part of the LNER system. This cross-country line lost its passenger service in the 1950s, and was completely closed by 1965.

Prior to the arrival of the 4-4-4Ts in 1920, main line passenger trains had been principally in the hands of the 0-4-4Ts, supplemented in 1915 by four 0-6-4Ts built by the Yorkshire Engine Company. The first of these, No.94 *Lord Aberconway*, is seen here at Neasden on 27 April 1927. They were the first Metropolitan engines to carry names since the original 4-4-0Ts Nos. 1-18 of 1864 and one or two miscellaneous shunting engines plus a couple of saddle tanks from the Brill branch. They were also destined to be the last.

Most of the 4-4-4Ts disappeared between 1942 and 1946, and only two survived to be renumbered under the later scheme, Nos.6416 and 6417 (Met Nos.104 and 105), which became Nos.7511 and 7512. These lasted until late 1947. No.7511 is at Colwick shed on 12 July 1947. All the others except No.6421 (scrapped in 1942) had been allocated the numbers 7510-7516, but never carried them.

No.96 *Charles Jones*, with an up train near Chorley Wood on 17 April 1935.

Charles Jones, renumbered LNER No.6156, with a freight train near Wendover on 8 July 1939.

Brill, in its new guise as LNER No.6157, at Chesham, 27 May 1939.

The fourth member of the quartet, *Robert H. Selbie,* Met No.95 and later LNER No.6155, was one of the two of the class which survived long enough to be renumbered under the 1946 scheme, when it became No.9076. This scene shows it under repair at Neasden LNER shed, 23 June 1948. This one, together with *Charles Jones,* were both withdrawn towards the end of 1948. *Brill* had gone some years before, in 1943, whilst *Lord Aberconway,* LNER No.6154 (although allocated No.9075), was scrapped in May 1946 as such. It was perhaps a little curious that the Metropolitan adopted two wheel arrangements not widely used in the British Isles, the 0-6-4T, and more particularly the 4-4-4T.

The last new engines for the Metropolitan Railway came in 1924 from Messrs Armstrong Whitworth & Co. There were six 2-6-4Ts, Nos.111-116, and incorporated parts of Maunsell S E & C R 2-6-0s built at Woolwich for war purposes, but which became surplus after the termination of hostilities. They were intended for freight duties, largely the conveyance of coal for Neasden power station from Verney Junction, at which point it was handed over by the LMS, from whence it had arrived from the Midlands. No.111 is seen at Aylesbury on 22 June 1935.

No.111 again, with an up freight running through Chorley Wood station on 2 June 1934.

No.116, with London Transport lettering, outside Neasden old shed, 11 July 1936.

No.112, also lettered London Transport, with an up freight near Chorley Wood on 17 August 1935.

The 2-6-4Ts were rarely to be found on passenger trains, but this view shows No.116 heading one near Chorley Wood on 5 June 1938.
 [E. R. Wethersett]

No.112 in the exchange sidings between the LMS and the Metropolitan, Verney Junction, 2 May 1936.

Nos.6159 and 6161 were scrapped in 1943; the remaining four were allocated Nos.9070-9073 under the 1946 renumbering scheme, but only two, 9070 (6158) and 9071 (6160) survived to carry them. The former is seen at Neasden (LNER) on 23 June 1948. Both of these survivors disappeared in October of that year.

In 1937 these engines became LNER Nos.6158–6163, and No.6160 (late No.113) is seen here at Neasden (former GCR) shed on 6 June 1946.

Two of a standard design of 0-6-0ST of Messrs Peckett & Sons of Bristol were obtained from that firm in 1897 and 1899, Met Nos. 101-102. One of their principal jobs was to shunt in Harrow goods yard, jointly owned by the Metropolitan and Great Central Railways, under an arrangement by which each of the two companies was responsible on an alternate basis for periods of five years. These two locomotives received no letter classification as applied to other classes. No.101 is in the usual immaculate condition of Metropolitan engines at this period; Neasden, 12 May 1934.

No.102 at Neasden on 11 July 1936 after being incorporated into the stock of the London Passenger Transport Board.

These two engines (Nos.101-102) later received the numbers L53 and L54 in the London Transport list. The former is seen here shunting at Neasden on 14 July 1939. They were scrapped in 1961-62.

The standard type of locomotive-hauled passenger stock used in later years was introduced in 1905, the first ten (Nos.419-428) appearing in that year, followed by Nos.429-448 in 1912 and finally 449-510, which appeared between 1920-1923. They were all of the ordinary compartment type; no lavatory facilities were provided, and they consisted of 7-compartment 1st class, 9-compartment 3rds, and 6 compartment 3rd brakes. Some of them were later incorporated into electric multiple units, and a few were scrapped during the war years, but 65 of them, made up into 5, 6 or 7 coach sets, remained in use until the end of locomotive-hauled trains in 1961. First class was abolished during the war, but in later years the discerning traveller was able to distinguish the former firsts, more roomy and comfortable, by the wider panels between the compartments. These views, taken at Aylesbury on 2 May 1936, show examples of the respective types, Nos.502, 431 and 496, the last mentioned, it will be noted, repainted 'London Transport'. Three of them, Nos.427, 465 and 509, are preserved on the Keighley & Worth Valley Railway.

Two early coaches survived on the Brill branch until closure in 1935. These were brake compartment thirds with rigid wheelbase, not bogies, as might appear at first sight. They were Nos.45 and 295, the last mentioned being seen here at Quainton Road on 8 April 1933.

Two of the magnificent coaches of the Pullman Car Company were obtained in 1910 to provide more luxurious facilities for businessmen on the morning and evening commuter trains to and from Verney Junction, Aylesbury, Chesham and Liverpool Street, as well as evening and late night theatre trains from Baker Street. These cars were *Galatea* and *Mayflower,* the latter being seen at Aylesbury on 2 May 1936. The service was not unnaturally discontinued under World War Two conditions, never to be resumed. The sight of such luxurious accommodation on the busy Inner Circle at underground stations like Moorgate and Farringdon would be difficult to visualise in this more austere and utilitarian age.

Miscellaneous non-passenger traffic over the main line of the Metropolitan called for the provision of such rolling stock as this horsebox, photographed at Wendover on 22 June 1935. Goods trains of course necessitated the conventional brake van, this picture being taken at Chalfont on 17 April 1935. Such vehicles have no place in the modern operation of London Transport. A milk van has been preserved, and is now at the London Transport Museum at Syon Park.

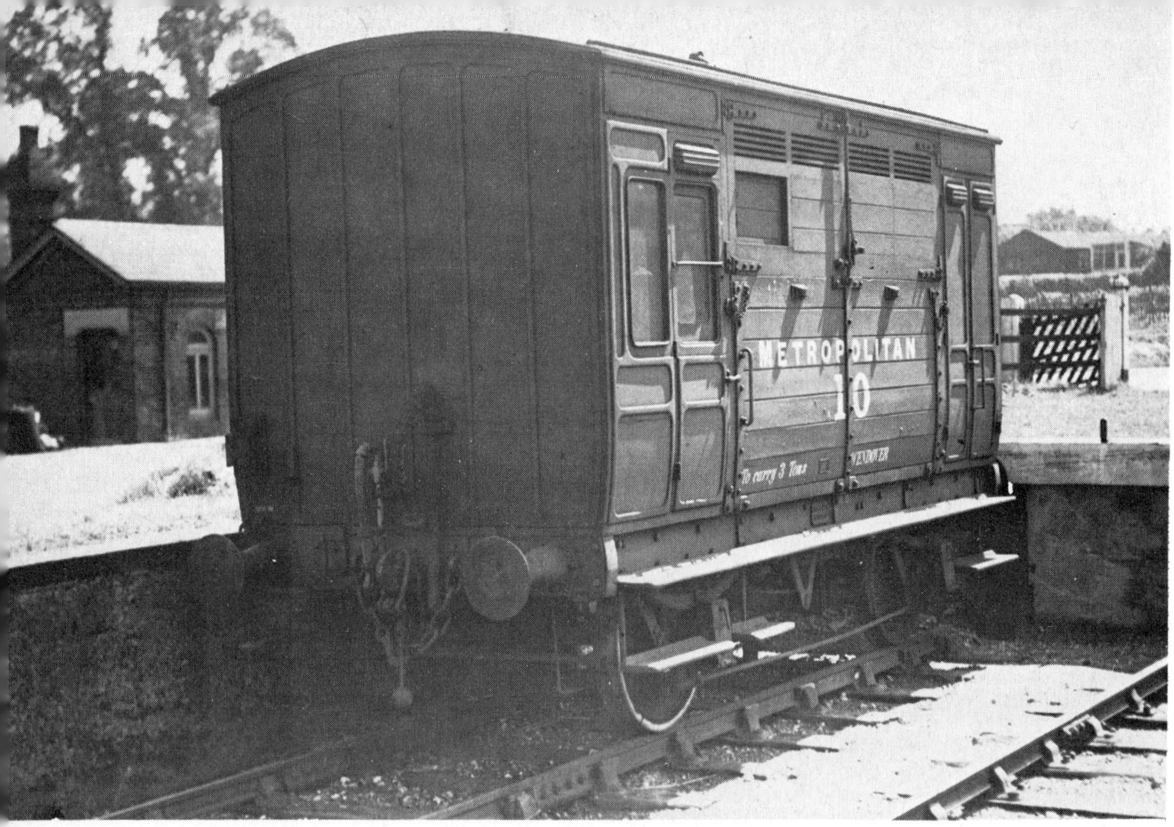
METROPOLITAN
10
To carry 3 Tons

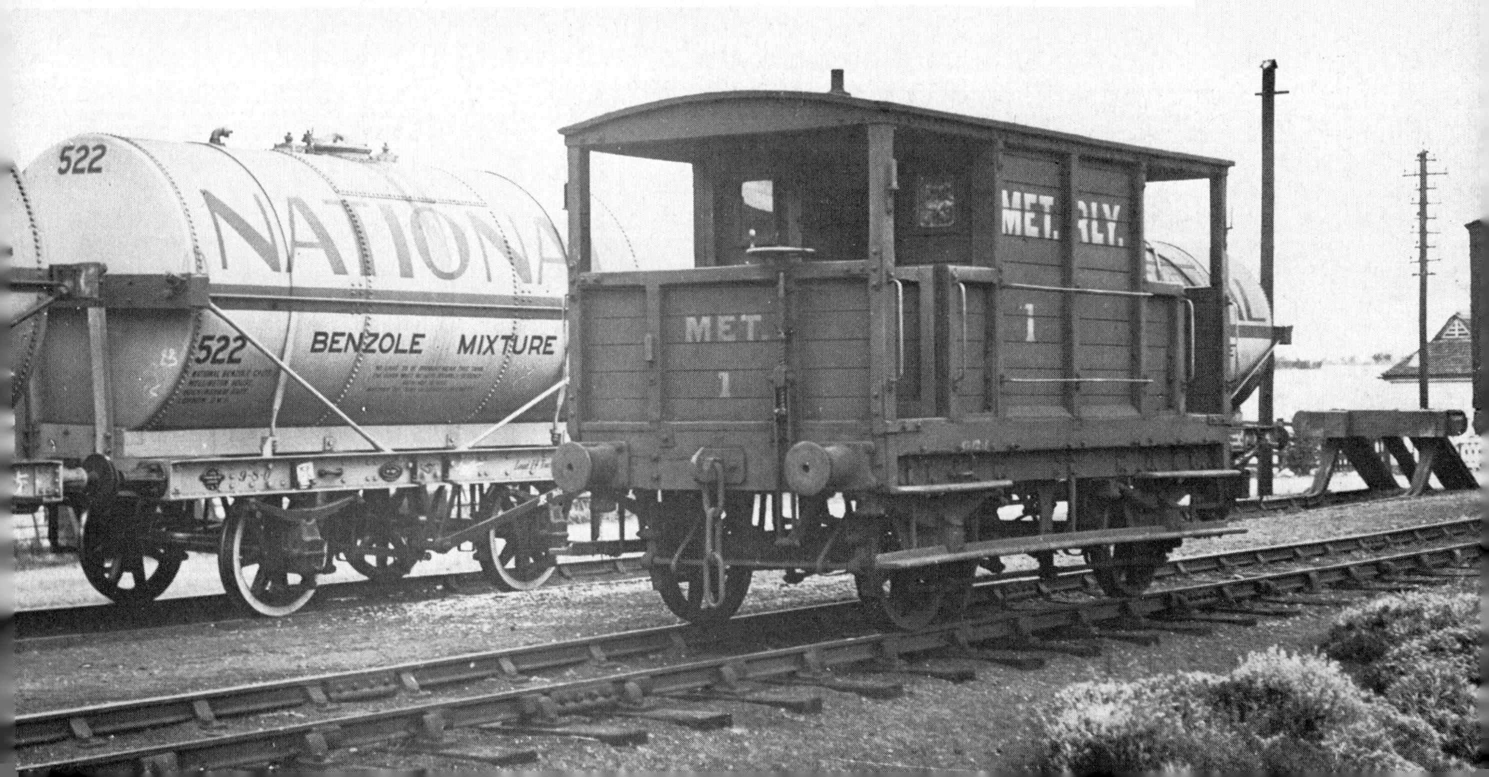
522
NATIONA
522
BENZOLE MIXTURE
MET. RLY.
MET.
1
1

Closely associated with the Metropolitan Railway, although entirely independent, was the Metropolitan District Railway which, in addition to its own lines in the eastern and western suburbs of London, also operated jointly with Metropolitan the southern half of the Inner Circle. The District went over to electric traction at the same time as the Metropolitan in 1905; this was obviously a necessity so far as the jointly operated Circle Line was concerned but it did not possess any outer country lines like the Met. and its whole passenger system was soon converted. Another similarity with the Met. was the use of the same type of Beyer Peacock 4-4-0Ts, of which two (Nos.33 and 34) were retained in later years for departmental use at the works at Lillie Bridge, adjacent to the West London Extension line at West Brompton. No.34 was photographed there on 12 August 1926, still largely in its original condition, together with a steam crane.

No.34 at the same location, 28 May 1931. Note that it has by now lost part of its condensing apparatus, the semi-circular pipe bridging the firebox, and has acquired a box-like cab. It has also reverted to the title 'District Railway', although in the earlier 1926 view it bore the legend 'UndergrounD'. When taken out of service in 1932, it was the last remaining example of a fleet which once consisted of 54 engines.

To replace the two 4-4-0Ts on departmental duties, a couple of 0-6-0Ts were obtained from the Hunslet Engine Co in 1931, numbered L30 and L31, the former being seen at Lillie Bridge on 28 May 1931. Both continued in service of the Transport Board until 1963.

To replace No.33, scrapped in 1925, one of the very similar engines was purchased from the Metropolitan Railway, No.22 on that line, and which thereupon became District No.35. This photograph was taken on 12 August 1926. No.35 was scrapped in 1931.

There was also a small 0-4-2ST built by Kerr Stuart & Co in 1922, thought to have been obtained second-hand. When photographed at Lillie Bridge on 28 May 1931 it was known as L33, although not carrying such identification, replacing the earlier 4-4-0T. It was scrapped about 1947.

53

The former erecting shop at Neasden works, on 11 March 1933. Visible is 4-4-0T No.23, under repair, which happens to be the one which has survived for preservation.

Another view in the works, taken on 11 July 1936. E class 0-4-4T No.77 has just been repainted in its new London Transport identity.

A view in Neasden loco yard, 11 July 1936. 2-6-4T No.116 is taking water while 4-4-4T No.103 awaits its turn. The coal stage is in the background, partly visible between Nos.116 and 105.

The old corrugated three-road shed at Neasden, 11 July 1936. This was demolished when the LNER took over the main line working and was replaced by a more modern building supplied to accommodate the few remaining steam engines.

The new shed, photographed on 4 October 1958; the second engine visible is the surviving 4-4-0T No.L45, then being retained for preservation. The power station can be seen in the background.

4-4-0T No.27 with breakdown train near Willesden Green, 10 May 1931. The separate LNER tracks to Marylebone are on the right.
[E. R. Wethersett]

The change-over from electric to steam at Rickmansworth; electric loco No.5 *John Hampden* has just arrived from Baker Street, 22 April 1933.

Two or three minutes later, it has been replaced by 4-4-4T No.103 to continue the journey to Aylesbury. Whilst no doubt desirable for the busy inner area on the outskirts of London, electrification was not considered necessary for the outer country districts, where the stations were anywhere between two and five miles apart. This cut down the necessity of frequent starting and stopping, and gave opportunities for considerable speeds between stations.

Another view, showing in particular the usual smart working of the change-over. Electric loco No.14 *Benjamin Disraeli,* having come off the train, has barely reversed on to the up line via the cross-over, before the waiting 4-4-4T, No.106, has emerged from the engine sidings to take over; 17 August 1935.

Former Metropolitan 2-6-4T No.9070 (with its first LNER number 6158 still to be seen on the buffer beam) also backing on to a train, 7 April 1947.

Another view of the Rickmansworth engine sidings, 7 April 1947. The LNER had by then taken over the steam working and two GCR 4-6-2Ts, Nos.9807 and 9808, are awaiting their turn to work a down train.

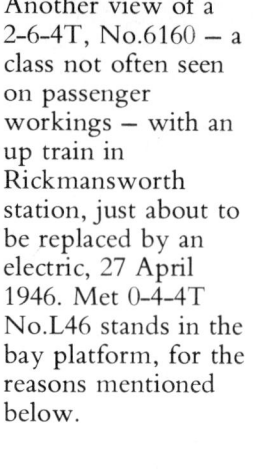

Another view of a 2-6-4T, No.6160 — a class not often seen on passenger workings — with an up train in Rickmansworth station, just about to be replaced by an electric, 27 April 1946. Met 0-4-4T No.L46 stands in the bay platform, for the reasons mentioned below.

During the early post-war period, Neasden (LNER) shed was short of serviceable engines owing to neglected standards of maintenance, and failures were so frequent that the Transport Board provided a spare locomotive as a stand-by during the busy evening period. This had perforce to be a Class E 0-4-4T, as they were the only passenger engines still available, and on several occasions they had to be called on to work down to Aylesbury — a duty on which they had not been seen since the arrival of the 4-4-4Ts back in 1920. No.L46 is waiting for such an emergency on 7 April 1947.

No.103, lettered 'London Transport', with a down train leaving Chorley Wood, 17 August 1935.

Chalfont and Latimer, junction for Chesham, 2 May 1936. The branch train standing in the bay platform is headed by Class E 0-4-4T No.81.

A train running into Chesham on 2 June 1934 with No.80 at its head.

No.1 in Chesham Station, 22 April 1933.

Although normally worked by a shuttle service, there were a few morning and evening trains to and from Baker Street or Liverpool Street. 4-4-4T No.110 stands in the run-around loop with one of these trains on 22 April 1933.

No.107 with an up train at Amersham in June 1935. This is now the terminal point of London Transport trains with electric multiple units, which took over on 9 September 1961. Great Missenden, Wendover, Stoke Mandeville and Aylesbury are now served by BR diesel multiple units from Marylebone.

An Aylesbury-Baker Street train at Stoke Mandeville, 2 May 1936.

Waddesdon station, between Aylesbury and Quainton Road, as seen from a down train, passing a motor train from Verney Junction, in May 1936. Prior to October 1922, this station was known as Waddesdon Manor. It was closed entirely in July 1936 and subsequently demolished. This section of the line no longer carries a passenger service.

The Brill branch platform on the same date as above. The whole area, apart from the through running line, had now been taken over by the Quainton Railway Society, and is the scene of considerable activity at weekends and public holidays during the summer season. Amongst the thirty or so engines now to be found there is Class E 0-4-4T No.L44 (originally Met No. 1, illustrated elsewhere in this volume) at present undergoing restoration.
[R. M. Casserley]

Quainton Road main platforms, looking south, 16 June 1957. Passenger services were discontinued in March 1963 and goods facilities in July 1966. A single line is still left in operation for freight trains between Aylesbury and Bletchley, by means of a spur to the LMR line at Calvert.
[R. M. Casserley]

4-4-0T No.23 on the level crossing at Wood Siding on the Brill branch, 22 June 1935.

Another view at the same location, with No.23 returning from Brill. This is a photograph which has been published before, but is repeated here for comparison with the lower view taken at the identical spot four years later (13 May 1939), the line having been abandoned since December 1935.

Waddesdon Road (not to be confused with Waddesdon; see page 70) on the Brill branch, 8 April 1933. To add slightly to the confusion, it may be added that prior to October 1922 this halt was just plain Waddesdon. Incidentally, both stations were situated in open countryside, a mile and more from the village they nominally served.

Brill shed, 15 March 1930. Engines normally spent a week at a time at this outpost, changing over with another of the class from Neasden at the weekend.

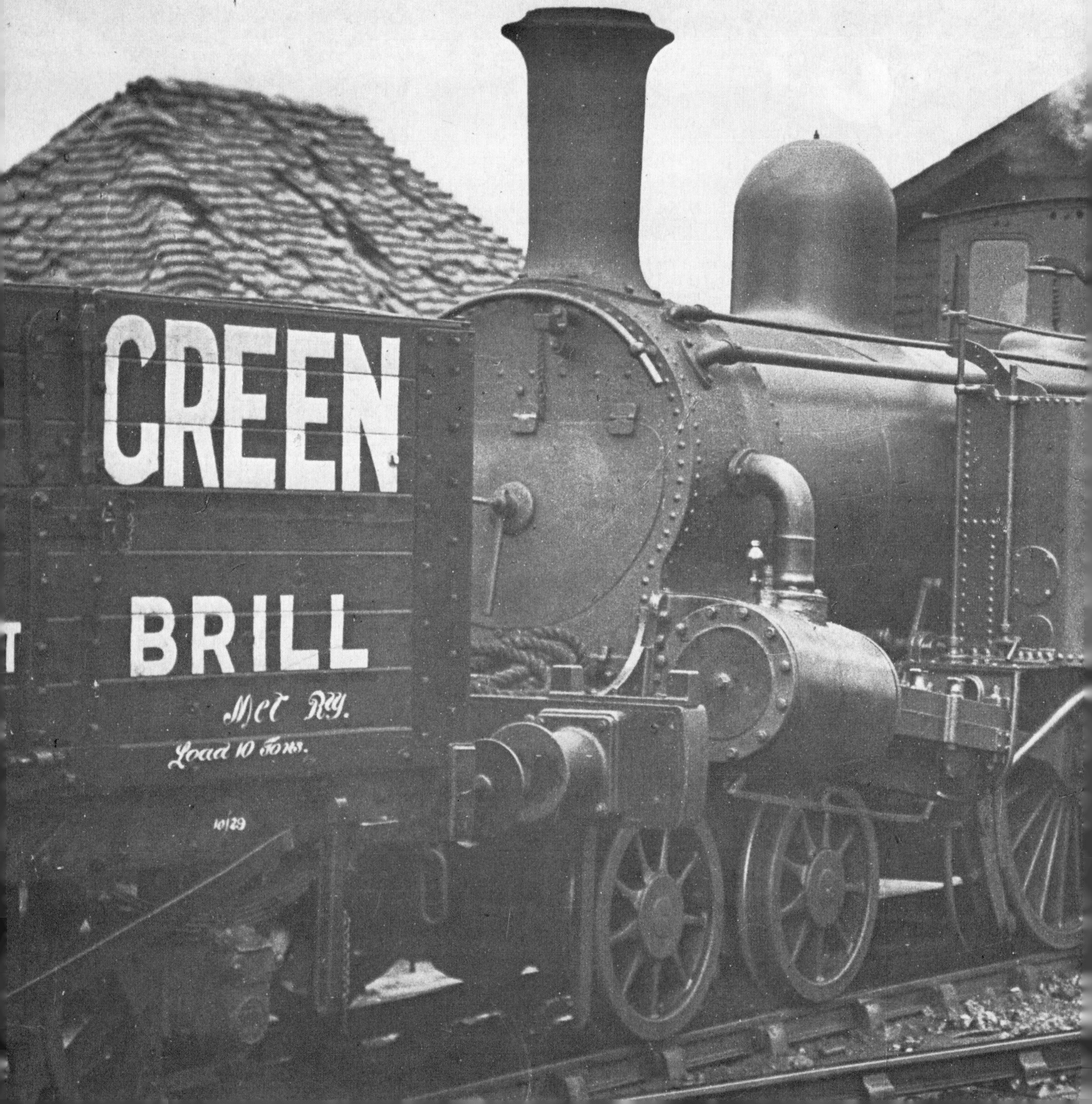

Quainton Road, March 1930, with pull-and-push train from Verney Junction with GCR F1 class 2-4-2T No.5594. The LNER operated a service of motor trains at this time between Verney Junction and Aylesbury to supplement the through Metropolitan trains to Baker Street.

Verney Junction, 2 May 1936. LNWR 2-4-2T No.6704 is in charge of a Bletchley to Oxford train, whilst in the background Metropolitan 4-4-4T No.107 waits to depart for Baker Street.

Winslow Road, between Quainton Road and Verney Junction, 2 May 1936. The motor train is in the hands of a former GER F7 2-4-2T, No.8307. Passenger services over this branch ceased in July 1936, and the line is now entirely abandoned.

As already mentioned, the LNER took over the working of main line trains north of Rickmansworth as from 1 November 1937, and acquired the Metropolitan engines of the G, H and K classes accordingly, which were transferred to the LNER shed at Neasden. Apart from the change of ownership, these continued to work the service for several years, but during the 1940s they were either withdrawn or, in the case of the 4-4-4Ts, sent north to the Nottingham area. They were replaced by LNER types, principally GCR 4-6-2Ts of Class A5, which had already been the mainstay of LNER outer suburban trains from Marylebone over the same route for many years. No.9807 is leaving Rickmansworth on 7 April 1947, having taken over a Met train from electric haulage at this point. The first six miles out to Amersham is almost continuous ascent of about 1 in 105, necessitating a good head of steam over the none-too-easy road through the Chiltern Hills, the heart of Metroland.

No.69823, repainted in early BR style, in the chalk cutting between Rickmansworth and Chorley Wood, 23 July 1949.

No.9808 with an up train running into Rickmansworth on the same day. The A5s used on the Metropolitan were almost entirely original Great Central engines, but Gresley also built thirteen further examples for use in the North Eastern area, with slight modifications, and classified class A/2. Two of these, Nos.1760 and 1766, worked from Neasden for a time between 1943 and 1945, when they were transferred back to Darlington.

No.5370 leaving Chalfont with an Aylesbury train on 30 March 1946; this was a rare appearance of one of the GCR L1 Class 2-6-4Ts, normally only seen on freight work.

Four Gresley 2-6-2Ts of Class V1 (Nos.407, 420, 424 and 446) appeared for a few months during 1943 on loan from Norwich, but they stayed only a short time before returning to that depot. It was not until 1948 that the A5s were replaced to any extent, when Thompson L1 2-6-4Ts began to appear. Sixteen of these were at Neasden by the end of that year; others followed later and they worked the Metropolitan trains for a considerable period until displaced by LM types, as recounted on the next pages. No.67794 is seen here with an up train entering Chalfont on 23 July 1935.

In 1958, consequent on the transfer of the Met and GC Joint line from the Eastern to the London Midland Region of British Railway, Neasden shed (hitherto coded 34E as a sub shed under the main LNER London area depot at Kings Cross) became 14D within the LMS group under the head depot, Cricklewood. As a result, former LMS types replaced the LNER L1s, which were sent away to other areas on that Region. The new influx consisted, so far as the working of the Met services were concerned, of 2-6-4Ts of Stanier and Fairburn design. In 1959 the allocation consisted of Nos.42080-2, 42086-42092, 42222/5, 42230-2, 42248-53/6, 42279, 42282-4, 42291, 42556, 42562/8, 42588, 42595, 42618, 42629 and 42674. No.42588 pauses at Rickmansworth on 3 January 1959. [R. M. Casserley]

No.42231 with an up train at Wendover, 26 July 1958.

Rather unusually, an earlier Fowler 2-6-4T, No.42338, was found leaving Great Missenden on 10 May 1958 with a train for Baker Street. None of this class was actually allocated to Neasden, this one being on temporary loan from Kentish Town shed.

In the last stage some BR Standard 2-6-4Ts found their way to Neasden, Nos.80137–80144, built at Brighton in 1956. These went new to this shed, where they remained until the end of steam working there in 1961, when they were transferred to the Southern. No.80144 on arrival at Rickmansworth, 29 August 1959, is about to be replaced by an electric loco. The pick-up shoes on the bogie of the end coaches next to the engine, as seen in this and other illustrations, served a double purpose, by bridging gaps in the current supply to the electric engine when traversing points and crossovers, and also to provide heating over the electrified section. The coaches were dual heated, with ordinary steam heating over the non-electrified lines beyond Rickmansworth.

For the Chesham branch, the LNER brought back from the north some GCR C13 4-4-2Ts, a type not seen in London since the earlier 1920s, when they were finally displaced from the Marylebone suburban services by A5 4-6-2Ts. Three of these, Nos.5002, 5115 and 5193 (later Nos.7420, 7438 and 7418), arrived in 1943. No.7438 was replaced by No.7416 in 1950. These remained until 1957/8 when they were in turn displaced by LMS type 2-6-2Ts. No.7420 is entering Chalfont with the Chesham branch train on 7 May 1947.

The Chesham branch through train from Liverpool Street leaving Chalfont on 30 March 1946 with No.5115 behind which it had worked from Rickmansworth.

Another former Great Central type which occasionally appeared on Metropolitan workings after 1937 was the N5 class 0-6-2T, of which several were stationed at Neasden, normally for shunting and local freight duties. The design actually dated back to Manchester, Sheffield & Lincolnshire days, having been introduced in 1891 and by the 1940s were amongst the oldest at work on the L N E R, at any rate in the London area. No.9257 (late L N E R No.5523) was photographed near Rickmansworth on 12 April 1947, with a through train from Baker Street to Chesham.

The GCR 4-4-2Ts on the motor-fitted Chesham shuttle service gave way in 1958 to LMS type 2-6-2Ts Nos.41270, 41272, 41284 and 41329. The last of these was photographed at Chesham on 3 June 1959. These trains were replaced by electric multiple units on 12 September 1960, the last steam train being worked by No.41284.
[R. M. Casserley]

An enthusiasts' special on 4 July 1954 included the Uxbridge branch in its itinerary to commemorate its 50th anniversary. Opened on 4 July 1904, the branch was electrically operated almost from the start, although for the first six months it had been steam worked. The special is seen here near Hillingdon.
[E. R. Wethersett]

Probably the only steam passenger train around the Inner Circle since electrification in 1905 was organised by the Stephenson Locomotive Society on 22 September 1957 and this scene shows the train about to leave Edgware Road with 0-4-4T No.L46. The 'ghost train' was viewed with almost incredulous amazement by passengers as it ran non-stop through the intermediate underground stations.

Special train leaving Amersham for Baker Street on 9 September 1961, the last day on which Metropolitan through services ran to and from Aylesbury, and after which locomotive-hauled trains ceased entirely.

The last steam-hauled passenger train ran on the Metropolitan on 1 October 1961. Organised by the Southern Counties Touring Society, this covered the Stanmore branch (which had been all-electric from the outset) to New Cross Gate via the East London line (see page 19). It is seen here approaching Farringdon from the north, behind 0-4-4T No.L44. The 'widened lines' will be noted on the right.

In 1956, London Transport began replacing its stock of remaining steam locomotives which it retained for departmental duties, by the purchase of former GWR 0-6-0PTs from British Railways, commencing with Nos.7711 and 5752, which became Nos.L90 and L91 in the LT loco list. Further engines of the same type were obtained up to 1963, by which date the last of the original Metropolitan locomotives and the two London Transport Hunslet engines of 1931, Nos.L30 and L31 (see page 53), were taken out of service. The two original GWR pannier tanks were later replaced by others, in all thirteen being obtained. The maximum number in service by 1963 was eleven (Nos.L89-L99) details being listed in the accompanying table. On withdrawal, several were sold to preservation societies and are still at work, but three remained in service with LT until May 1971, when they were replaced by diesel-hydraulic locomotives. This was the end of steam working, and it is interesting to note that it survived three years longer than on British Railways itself. Another curious historical fact was that Metropolitan steam finished as it had begun, by the use of Great Western engines — the first trains over the newly-opened line between Paddington and Farringdon in January 1863 having been worked by GWR broad gauge 2-4-0Ts of the design of Daniel Gooch. A final commemorative steam special was run on Sunday 6 June 1971 from Moorgate over the 'widened' lines through Farringdon, and the circle line to Baker Street, thence to Neasden where it terminated. This train was composed of departmental vehicles and no passengers could be carried as there was no longer any suitable coaching stock available, but its journey was witnessed by several hundred spectators at the intermediate stations. It was hauled by 0-6-0PT No.94 and three days later this engine was despatched to Tyseley Steam Centre, for preservation, where it has since been restored as GWR No.7752.

Particulars of GWR 0-6-0PTs purchased from British Railways

LT No	GWR No.	Year of purchase	Disposal
L90 (first)	7711	1956	Scrapped 1961 and replaced, see below.
L91 (first)	5752	1956	Scrapped 1960 and replaced, see below.
L92	5786	1958	To Worcester Loco Soc, Hereford 1969
L93	7779	1958	Scrapped 1968
L94	7752	1959	To Tyseley Steam Centre, 1971
L91 (second)	5757	1960	Scrapped 1968
L95	5764	1960	To Severn Valley Rly.,1971
L96	7741	1961	Scrapped 1967
L90 (second)	7760	1961	To Tyseley Steam Centre, 1971
L97	7749	1962	Scrapped 1970
L98	7739	1962	Scrapped 1970
L99	7715	1963	To Quainton Rd Society, 1969
L89	5775	1963	To Keighley & Worth Valley Railway, 1969

Styles of restoration of the preserved engines vary; most have been repainted in GWR or BR liveries with their former numbers in the form of GWR-type number plates, but No.L89 on the K&WVR retains its London Transport identity. Although at the time of writing it is in yellow-brown livery, it may revert to London Transport maroon.

The illustration shows the first No.L90 at Neasden in October 1958.

Fortunately two Metropolitan engines have survived for preservation. No.23, one of the original Beyer Peacock tanks, at first found a resting place in Clapham Museum, as seen here in May 1970, restored to its original condition. Later it was moved to the London Transport Museum at Syon Park (Brentford), opened in 1973. The other survival is 0-4-4T No.L44, featured in more than one illustration in this volume. This was formerly Metropolitan No.1, now owned by the Quainton Railway Society, and currently being restored at their premises at Quainton Road.